Promises *to* Encourage Your Soul

Inspirational Refreshment for Your Spirit

Promises *to* Encourage Your Soul

Inspirational Refreshment for Your Spirit

BARBOUR

Published by Barbour Publishing, Inc., P.O. Box 719, Uhrichsville, Ohio 44683, www.barbourbooks.com

Our mission is to publish and distribute inspirational products offering exceptional value and biblical encouragement to the masses.

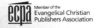 Member of the
Evangelical Christian
Publishers Association

Printed in China.

Contents

INTRODUCTION

BE ENCOURAGED!

*May our Lord Jesus Christ himself and God our Father. . .
encourage your hearts and strengthen you.*
2 THESSALONIANS 2:16–17 NIV

*S*ome days we need a gentle hand to pick us up and a voice to whisper encouragement in our ears. Life can be challenging, and when trials come our way, we may feel discouraged. But God does not fail us, no matter what our days hold. His Word provides comfort for all our troubles.

~Pamela McQuade

Blessings

"Blessed be the name of God forever and ever, for wisdom and might are His."

DANIEL 2:20 NKJV

Unappreciated Blessings?

When God brings us through a trial, do we worship Him with great thankfulness or do we take that blessing as our due? Though God is great, He doesn't appreciate being taken for granted any more than we would.

Required to describe King Nebuchadnezzar's bad dream to him or face imminent death, Daniel didn't worry or have a pity party. Instead, he called a prayer meeting of his three best friends. In the middle of the night, God answered their prayers, revealing Nebuchadnezzar's dream to Daniel, the wisest of the Babylonian king's wise men.

Daniel's first and very grateful response, in the midst of his relief, was to praise the Lord who had saved his life. He gave God recognition for His saving grace even before he went to see the king who had threatened to kill him.

We may believe that our Lord answers in such life-and-death situations, but do we have confidence He takes care of smaller troubles, too? And when He does respond to an ordinary situation, do we give thanks?

~Pamela McQuade

When we lose one blessing, another is often most unexpectedly given in its place.

C. S. LEWIS

Mary's Song of Praise

*L*ord, of all the women in the world—young or old, rich or poor, of high status or low—You chose a young girl from an unimportant, backwater province to bear Your Son, our Savior. Her response was, appropriately, a song of joy and praise, one of the most moving prayers in the Bible. Mary understood that You had given her a great honor that would be remembered forever, and she welcomed it—as well as the responsibility that came with it—with joy. You bless my life in many ways every day, Father. May I receive Your blessings with a song of thanksgiving on my lips.

~Toni Sortor

"I am coming to you now, but I say these things while I am still in the world, so that they may have the full measure of my joy within them."

John 17:13 NIV

Just Half a Cup

*J*ust half a cup, please." A friend is offered a cup of piping hot coffee, but she declines a full cup, accepting only a small amount. Perhaps she is trying to be polite, or maybe she feels as though she's had enough coffee already that day. But it is difficult and unnatural for her friend to stop pouring at half a cup, so she pours just a bit more than what was requested. She wants to give her friend the fullest possible measure of enjoyment that she can in that one cup of coffee.

That's how our Father feels when He longs to bestow His richest blessings and wisdom on us. He loves us, so He desires to fill our cup to overflowing with the things that He knows will bring us pleasure and growth. Do you tell Him to stop pouring when your cup is only half full? You may not even realize it, but perhaps your actions dictate that your cup remain half empty. Seek a full cup, and enjoy the full measure of the joy of the Lord.

~Nicole O'Dell

Never lose an opportunity of seeing anything that is beautiful; for beauty is God's handwriting— a wayside sacrament. Welcome it in every fair face, in every fair sky, in every fair flower, and thank God for it as a cup of blessing.

RALPH WALDO EMERSON

God's Mercy

*F*ather God, Mary realized that her honor was not of her own making but came as a gift from You. All she had done was live in obedience to Your laws the best she could, as had her fathers and those before them since Abraham. You had promised to do mighty things for Your people. Sometimes they had obeyed You and flourished; other times they had followed idols and felt the pain of Your anger. However, Your mercy is always on those who follow You, and their blessings flow from Your constant love. Make me mindful of Your great gifts, Father, that my song may praise Your work in my life.

~Toni Sortor

For he that is mighty hath done to me great things;
and holy is his name. And his mercy is on them
that fear him from generation to generation.

LUKE 1:49–50 KJV

Comfort & Contentment

But godliness with contentment is great gain.

1 TIMOTHY 6:6 KJV

CONTENTMENT IN CHRIST

*I*n the midst of a conversation, the young woman was caught short.

"Will you ever be content?" her friend asked.

"I don't know," she said. "I don't think so. I always want things to be better than they are."

The question echoed as the years passed. A career melted into marriage and motherhood. With each challenge, she worked harder to make things better. Nevertheless, she often felt empty. She wondered if there was a better way to live.

There is. True profit and gain lie not in toiling for money but in being content with one's situation.

How can we learn contentment?

We must start looking to Jesus. If we take hold of all we have as joint heirs with Christ and as partakers of grace, we will have no desire for the world's riches.

According to the Bible, we are raised up with Jesus and are seated in the heavenly places with Him. We have His constant presence through the indwelling Holy Spirit. He has given us all things that pertain unto life and godliness. What more do we need?

We need a fresh vision for who we are in Christ. Therein we will find contentment.

~Helen Middlebrooke

The thought of You stirs us so deeply that we cannot be content unless we praise You, because You have made us for Yourself, and our hearts find no peace until they rest in You.

SAINT AUGUSTINE

COVETOUSNESS

*I*t is so easy to fall into the trap of covetousness, Lord. Today everything is bigger, better, new and improved. About the only thing that doesn't get repackaged every year is Ivory soap, but that still gets me clean. I miss old-fashioned contentment, using time-proven products, and watching the sun set instead of the evening news. Still, I admit I am not totally content. There's just so much available, and some of it looks pretty good. On days when a commercial gets to me a little, remind me that I have everything I really need, Lord. Best of all, I have You, whose promises never change, and You will always supply my true needs.

~Toni Sortor

She thought, "If I just touch his clothes,
I will be healed."

MARK 5:28 NIV

REACH OUT AND TOUCH

We should never underestimate the power of touch. In our busy lives, as we rush from one appointment to another, skimping on affection with our families and loved ones can become routine. We wave good-bye to our children without stopping for a hug. Husbands head off to work with the barest brush of a kiss.

We do our loved ones a disservice, however, when we skip touching them. Touching communicates our affection but also our affirmation and sympathy. You can encourage people—or comfort them—with a simple touch. The Bible records Jesus touching many people, comforting and healing them. He also let people touch Him, such as the sinful woman who touched and kissed His feet (Luke 7:38).

In Mark 5, however, the true power of a simple touch is beautifully portrayed. This woman who had suffered for so long believed so strongly in Jesus that she knew the quickest touch of His hem would heal her. She reached out, and her faith made her well.

So hold those you love close. Hug them, and let them see a bit of Jesus' love in you every day.

~Ramona Richards

God is everything that is good and comfortable for us.
He is our clothing that for love wraps us, clasps us,
and all surrounds us for tender love.

JULIAN OF NORWICH

AFFLICTION

I have been afflicted in my lifetime, as have most women, but You helped me walk out of affliction and invited me to Your continual feast. Right now I am still at Your banquet, but I know affliction will come again. I am content and comfortable, enjoying life to its fullest. I don't know if I will feel that way when trials come to me again, because I don't really have a merry heart. Like most people, I am happiest when things are going nicely, but when things go wrong, my heart is not so merry. Help me get over this nagging self-doubt, Father. Remind me that Your blessings are forever and I have nothing to fear. Give me a merry heart, I pray.

~Toni Sortor

*Be content with such things as ye have: for he hath said,
I will never leave thee, nor forsake thee.*

HEBREWS 13:5 KJV

Hope

I pray that God, the source of hope, will fill you completely with joy and peace because you trust in him. Then you will overflow with confident hope through the power of the Holy Spirit.

ROMANS 15:13 NLT

GOD OF HOPE

*I*n our busy, fast-paced lives, we may feel exhausted at times. Our culture fosters frenzy and ignores the need for rest and restoration. Constantly putting out fires and completing tasks, working incessantly, we may feel discouraged and disheartened with life. There is more to life than this, isn't there?

Our God of hope says, "*Yes!*" God desires to fill us to the brim with joy and peace. But to receive this gladness, rest, and tranquillity, we need to have faith in the God who is trustworthy and who says, "Anything is possible if a person believes" (Mark 9:23 NLT). We need to place our confidence in God who, in His timing and through us, will complete that task, mend that relationship, or do whatever it is we need. The key to receiving and living a life of hope, joy, and peace is recounting God's faithfulness out loud, quietly in your heart, and to others. When you begin to feel discouraged, exhausted, and at the end of your rope, *stop*; go before the throne of grace and recall God's faithfulness.

~Tina C. Elacqua

We walk without fear, full of hope and courage and strength to do His will, waiting for the endless good which He is always giving as fast as He can get us able to take it in.

GEORGE MACDONALD

ANXIETY

Generalized anxiety, the doctors call it—that nagging feeling that something is wrong but cannot be pinned down. A lot of women know this feeling. It seems to be our job to worry about others and see dangers others never glimpse. Yet You did not create me to live in fear but in hope. It is Your joy to watch over me, Father. Who could do it better? You are with my husband on the long drive to work. You hold my child's hand at the crosswalk. I am not responsible for everyone and everything—You are, and I know You are trustworthy. Help me to hope in You and trust Your protection.

~Toni Sortor

*Keep your eyes on Jesus, who both began
and finished this race we're in.*

HEBREWS 12:2 MSG

REMEMBER THIS

*I*t can happen in a split second. Your life is suddenly turned upside down. Your mother is rushed to the emergency room. Your doctor utters the word "cancer." Layoffs leave you jobless. Dark clouds quickly obscure your vision. Emotions reel out of control. Questions without answers rush through your mind. Life has been dramatically altered in the blink of an eye.

If you have not encountered such an experience, it's likely that someday you will. Prepare yourself now. Remember that when life throws us curveballs, we may be caught off guard, but God never is. He knows all things: past, present, and future. Since He knows what lies ahead, He can safely navigate us through the chaos.

When our heads are spinning and tears are flowing, there is only one thing to remember: Focus on Jesus. He will never leave you nor forsake you. When you focus on Him, His presence envelops you. Where there is despair, He imparts hope. Where there is fear, He imparts faith. Where there is worry, He imparts peace. He will lead you on the right path and grant you wisdom for the journey. When the unexpected trials of life come upon you, remember this: Focus on Jesus.

~Julie Rayburn

Life is what we are alive to. It is not length but breadth. . . . Be alive to. . .goodness, kindness, purity, love, history, poetry, music, flowers, stars, God, and eternal hope.

MALTBIE D. BABCOCK

EVIDENCE

*L*ord, astronomers have recently discovered distant moons and planets they cannot see through even the strongest of telescopes. By observing the effects these bodies have on other bodies—changes in orbit, for example—they know these distant bodies simply *must* be there or their effects would not be there. This is "evidence of things not seen," perhaps even the "substance of things hoped for." I admit I do not totally understand how the astronomers do this, but I find it comforting. There is so much I do not understand about You. Still, I can see the effects of Your actions, the evidence that You are still active in my daily life and the lives of others. I do not need to physically see You to believe. Your evidence is everywhere.

~Toni Sortor

Why art thou cast down, O my soul? and why art thou disquieted within me? hope thou in God: for I shall yet praise him, who is the health of my countenance, and my God.

PSALM 42:11 KJV

Joy

And even though you do not see [Jesus] now,
you believe in him and are filled with an inexpressible
and glorious joy, for you are receiving the goal of
your faith, the salvation of your souls.

1 PETER 1:8–9 NIV

Joy Is Jesus

As children we find joy in the smallest things: a rose in bloom, a ladybug at rest, the circles a pebble makes when dropped in water. Then somewhere between pigtails and pantyhose, our joy wanes and eventually evaporates in the desert of difficulties.

But when we find Jesus, "all things become new" as the Bible promises, and once again, we view the world through a child's eyes. Excitedly we experience the "inexpressible and glorious joy" that salvation brings.

We learn that God's joy isn't based on our circumstances; rather, its roots begin with the seed of God's Word planted in our hearts. Suddenly our hearts spill over with joy, knowing that God loves and forgives us and that He is in complete control of our lives. We have joy because we know this world is not our permanent home and a mansion awaits us in glory.

Joy comes as a result of whom we trust, not in what we have. Joy is Jesus.

~Tina Krause

To be a joy-bearer and a joy-giver says everything;
for in our life, if one is joyful, it means that one is
faithfully living for God and that nothing else counts;
and if one gives joy to others, one is doing God's work;
with joy without and joy within, all is well.

JANET ERSKINE STUART

ACCEPTING THE GIFT

*L*ord, You know that sometimes I reject Your promises. When I am really lonely and depressed, nothing seems to make me feel better. I know You are with me; I know You care when no one else cares—but some days even that is not enough. The fault is in me, not in You. On days like that, remind me that although Your promises are free for the taking, I still need to accept them, to claim them, and then to live in faith that they are mine. No gift is truly ours until we open it and accept it in thankfulness and joy.

~Toni Sortor

*"Do not grieve, for the joy of the
LORD is your strength."*

NEHEMIAH 8:10 NIV

Desert Flower

*F*riday dawned gloomy and overcast. *A fitting end to a miserable week,* Cheryl thought. Her husband had wrecked the car, and her daughter had broken her thumb in a tumble at school. A beloved friend had been diagnosed with an aggressive form of uterine cancer.

As Cheryl stared at a sky the color of bruises, she blinked back tears and fell to her knees. Second Timothy 4:6 (NIV) came to mind: "I am already being poured out like a drink offering." She could relate to Paul's expression of helplessness. Cheryl felt empty. She cried out to the Lord; then she just cried.

And a strange thing happened. A sensation of warmth started in her toes and spread throughout her body, infusing her with something totally unexpected—joy! She enjoyed a refreshing time of praise-filled fellowship with the Renewer of her soul.

Not to be confused with happiness, joy is not dependent on external circumstances. It's a Holy Spirit–inspired mystery that defies all reason. During the times we should be downcast or depressed, the joy of the Lord bolsters us like a life preserver in a tumultuous sea.

Living joyfully is not denying reality. We all have hurts in our lives. But even in the midst of our parched desert times, our heavenly Father reaches in with gentle fingers to lift and sustain us.

~Debora M. Coty

Where the soul is full of peace and joy,
outward surroundings and circumstances
are of comparatively little account.

HANNAH WHITALL SMITH

THE PROMISE

*P*eter was surrounded by people asking what they must do to receive the Holy Spirit. His answer was simple: "Repent, and be baptized. . .for the remission of sins" (Acts 2:38 KJV). This promise was given to all, from every nation, of every status, near or far, adults and children alike. You, Lord, will do the calling; all we need to do is repent and be baptized. The process is simple so that even the simplest can understand. Help me explain this to my children, Lord. I yearn to know they belong to You, for as John said, "I have no greater joy than to hear that my children walk in truth" (3 John 4 KJV).

~Toni Sortor

For the promise is unto you, and to your children,
and to all that are afar off, even as many
as the Lord our God shall call.

ACTS 2:39 KJV

Love

Jesus replied: " 'Love the Lord your God with all your heart and with all your soul and with all your mind.' This is the first and greatest commandment. And the second is like it: 'Love your neighbor as yourself.' "

MATTHEW 22:37–39 NIV

CONVENIENT LOVE

Christians have been given two assignments: Love God and love each other.

People say love is a decision. Sounds simple enough, right? The fact is that telling others we love them and showing that love are two very different realities. Let's face it—some people are harder to love than others. Even loving and serving God seem easier on a less stressful day.

Think about convenience stores. They're everywhere. Why? Because along the journey, people need things. It's nearly impossible to take a long road trip without stopping. Whether it's gas to fill our vehicles, a quick snack, or a drink to quench thirsty lips, everyone needs something. Gas station owners realize this, and we should, too.

It may not always be convenient to love God when the to-do list stretches on forever or when a friend asks us for a favor that takes more time than we want to give. But God's love is available 24/7. He never puts us on hold or doles out love in rationed amounts. He never takes a day off, and his love is plentiful.

~Kate E. Schmelzer

After the verb "to love"..."to help" is the most beautiful verb in the world.

BERTHA VON SUTTNER

Working for God's Glory

In the end, Father, You will be the judge of my lifetime of work, and I know You don't care if I work behind a cash register or an oak desk with a five-line telephone. It's not what I do that matters, but how I do it. Am I a cheerful worker? Am I an honest worker? Am I a worker whose love for You is evident in what I say and how I treat my fellow workers? Do I care more for my brothers and sisters than for my next paycheck? I am Your ambassador, Lord, and every day I try to show Your love to those who do not know You. I pray that when the time comes, You will find me worthy.

~Toni Sortor

*"When Israel was a child, I loved him,
and out of Egypt I called my son."*

HOSEA 11:1 NIV

OUT OF EGYPT

When we think of these words in Hosea 11:1, it is usually in connection to Jesus, as God called Him out of Egypt after Herod's death. But read the verse after it, and you will discover God's condemnation of His wandering people. Though God called Israel with love, they turned aside from Him to pagan worship.

Scripture often holds similar surprises. An uplifting verse is followed by one that speaks of deep sin. God's promises and humanity's sin run together in entwined messages.

Isn't that just the way the Christian life is? God's merciful thread runs through our pain-filled, erroneous lives. Like a bright, gold line, it brightens our existence and begins to turn us from sin-filled ore to bright, pure gold.

For not only did God call His Son from Egypt, He calls us, too, to leave behind the darkness of sin and live in His holiness. His love strips evil from us and brings us into close relationship to Him.

God has called you out of Egypt because He loves you. Love Him in return.

~Pamela McQuade

Love comforteth like sunshine after rain.

WILLIAM SHAKESPEARE

Hold My Hand

*O*ften I am like a little child in a big toy store, running from aisle to aisle and asking for everything that looks good. Sometimes You grant me my wish; other times You say no. Like a loving parent, You hold me by the hand so I don't get lost in the store, just as my mother always did. Like my mother, You point out when my wishes are poorly made or too expensive for my soul. I admit that once in a while I have a temper tantrum, disputing Your guidance and wanting my own way, but You have never been wrong. Thank You for Your love and patience, for I will always need Your guidance, Lord.

~Toni Sortor

I am continually with thee: thou hast holden me by my right hand. Thou shalt guide me with thy counsel, and afterward receive me to glory.

PSALM 73:23–24 KJV

Prayer

Hear my prayer, O Lord,
and let my cry come to You.

PSALM 102:1 NKJV

Trust Test

Have you had days when your prayers seemed to hit the ceiling and bounce back? Does God seem distant for no reason you're aware of? Chances are good that if you've been a Christian for more than a short time, you've experienced this.

The psalmist experienced it as pain and suffering became his lot. At night insomnia plagued him. During his tired days, enemies taunted him. His was a weary life, and in earthly terms, he hardly could see the outcome.

But once the psalmist described his plight, his psalm turned in a new direction, glorifying God. Suddenly life wasn't so bad anymore, because he trusted in the One who would save him.

When prayer hits the ceiling, it's time to remind ourselves of God's greatness, not complain about what we think He hasn't done. As we face trials that threaten to undo us, let's remind ourselves that He has not forgotten us and our ultimate security is never at risk.

As we feel the dangers of life, let's trust that God is still listening to our prayers. He will never fail us. All He asks is that our reliance on Him remains firm. At the right hour, we'll feel His love again.

~Pamela McQuade

*I have been driven many times to my knees
by the overwhelming conviction that I
had absolutely no other place to go.*

ABRAHAM LINCOLN

Elisabeth

Zacharias and Elisabeth had waited years for a child, and now they both were old, well past the age for bearing children, no matter how much they wanted one. Then Gabriel, Your messenger, appeared to Zacharias with the good news that the son Elisabeth would bear would prepare the way for the coming of Your Son.

Father, sometimes it seems my deepest desires will never bear fruit, no matter how much I pray. I go on with my life, but there is an emptiness in my heart that only You can fill. I know not all prayers are answered, but many are, so I continue to petition You, for You are my hope.

~Toni Sortor

*But the angel said unto him. Fear not,
Zacharias: for thy prayer is heard;
and thy wife Elisabeth shall bear thee a son,
and thou shalt call his name John.*

Luke 1:13 kjv

AVAILABLE 24/7

No one is available to take your call at this time, so leave a message and we will return your call—or not—if we feel like it. . .and only between the hours of 4:00 and 4:30 p.m. Thank you for calling. Have a super day!

We've all felt the frustration of that black hole called voice mail. It is rare to reach a real, honest-to-goodness, breathing human being the first time we dial a telephone number.

Fortunately our God is always available. He can be reached at any hour of the day or night and every day of the year—including weekends and holidays! When we pray, we don't have to worry about disconnections, hang-ups, or poor reception. We will never be put on hold or our prayers diverted to another department. The Bible assures us that God is eager to hear our petitions and that He welcomes our prayers of thanksgiving. The psalmist David wrote of God's response to those who put their trust in Him: "He will call upon me, and I will answer him" (Psalm 91:15 NIV). David had great confidence that God would hear his prayers. And we can, too!

~Austine Keller

Pray, and let God worry.

MARTIN LUTHER

Gabriel and Mary

Gabriel told Mary that she would bear a child by the Holy Ghost—Jesus, the Savior the Jews had waited for. Then he gave her the news that her barren cousin Elisabeth was also pregnant, despite her age. Gabriel's using Elisabeth as an example of Your power must have eased Mary's mind, especially when he concluded, "For with God nothing shall be impossible" (Luke 1:37 KJV). Quite often I pray for what I know is impossible, Lord. I know that in the best of all worlds, most of my prayers will not be realized. But some will, if they are in Your will for me. For You, nothing is impossible.

~Toni Sortor

I call on you, O God, for you will answer me;
give ear to me and hear my prayer.

PSALM 17:6 NIV

Strength

By his divine power, God has given us everything we need for living a godly life.

2 Peter 1:3 nlt

ARE YOU GETTING SQUEEZED?

Does your schedule ever get so full you feel like you can't breathe? Maybe your boss demands meeting on top of meeting, or your children's extracurricular activities have you going in circles. Somehow you keep moving forward, not always sure where the strength comes from but thankful in the end that you made it through the day.

In those situations, you're not just stretching your physical body to the limit but your mind and emotions as well. Stress can make you feel like a grape in a winepress. The good news is that God has given you everything you need, but it's up to you to utilize the wisdom He has provided. Don't be afraid to say no when you feel you just can't add one more thing to your to-do list. Limit your commitments, ask someone to take notes for you in a meeting you can't make, or carpool with someone who shares your child's extracurricular activity.

Alleviate the pressure where you can, and then know that God's power will make up for the rest.

~Shanna Gregor

If God sends us on stony paths,
he provides strong shoes.

CORRIE TEN BOOM

OUR SOURCE OF STRENGTH

On my own, I am rarely as strong as I need to be, Lord. Sickness weakens me; cares and worry tire my mind and make me less productive than I want to be. Old age will eventually defeat my body. Even when I am physically fit, I know there is weakness in me. But You promise that I will be able to continue in Your way as long as I have faith, and I trust Your promises. Make me stronger every day, Lord, no matter how heavy my burdens may be. Show me all the good You have done for the faithful throughout history, and give me some of Your strength when my own fails. Let my dependence on You turn weakness into strength.

~Toni Sortor

"I will make a pathway through the wilderness.
I will create rivers in the dry wasteland."

ISAIAH 43:19 NLT

Mountains out of Molehills

*S*ome days mountains of work are piled in front of us. Whether they consist of schoolwork, diapers, dirty laundry, business reports, or all of the above, the height of such tasks can sometimes seem to be overwhelming. We don't even know where to begin. Immediately the enemy begins whispering in our ears, "Good luck trying to get all that done. You don't have a chance. And if you try to rush through it, no one will be happy with the results. Especially not you."

These are the times when we need to take stock of the situation. First things first. Don't panic! Take a deep breath. Tell yourself that you can do all things with Christ's strength (see Philippians 4:13). You have God's Word on it. Send up a prayer for strength. Then just simply do the next thing. Take the first step.

Although situations sometimes seem impossible, we have a God—a great big, mighty God—who makes a way in the wilderness for us. He can *move* mountains. Nothing will stop Him from helping us—except maybe ourselves and a negative mind-set. Do not doubt. But take that first step forward, knowing He will make a way where there seems to be no way.

~Donna K. Maltese

Our strength grows out of our weaknesses.

RALPH WALDO EMERSON

Both Full and Hungry

The troubles I am having are nothing compared to what Paul went through, yet You taught him great lessons. "I know both how to be abased, and I know how to abound: every where and in all things I am instructed both to be full and to be hungry, both to abound and to suffer need" (Philippians 4:12 KJV). The result of his education was "I can do all things through Christ which strengtheneth me" (v. 13). Some of Your lessons are painful, Lord, but I struggle to absorb them, to learn from them, and to come through them a more complete person. The fact that I do abound sometimes is easier to take, but even that lesson has its costs. May I learn to appreciate all that life offers, knowing there is profit in both the easy and hard times.

~Toni Sortor

I can do all things through Christ
which strengtheneth me.

PHILIPPIANS 4:13 KJV

Trials

*Give thanks to the LORD, for he is good;
his love endures forever.*

PSALM 107:1 NIV

Steadfast Love

When the sea of life batters us, it's easy to forget the Lord's goodness. Caught up in our own storms, tunnel vision afflicts us as we view the troubles before us and may doubt the Lord whom we serve. Though we might not consciously separate ourselves from Him, deep inside we fear He won't act to save us—or that He won't act in time.

That's a good time to stop and give thanks to God, who never stops being good or ends His love for us. Our situations change, our love fails, but God never varies. He entirely controls all creation, and His character never changes. The darkest circumstances we face will not last eternally. Life moves on and alters. But God never deserts us.

Even when our troubles seem to be in control, they aren't. God has not changed, and our doubts cannot make alterations in Him. If we allow faith to take control, we will realize that and turn again to Him.

Facing troubles? Give thanks to the Lord. He is good. He hasn't deserted you, no matter what you face, and His goodness will never end. He won't fail us.

~Pamela McQuade

By trials God is shaping us for higher things.

HENRY WARD BEECHER

MY DEFENSE

No matter what befalls me in my lifetime, my defenses remain strong in times of trouble. They are not the defenses of an armed force, as necessary as that may be from time to time; they are the safety of Your promises and the assurance of Your mighty protection. Times do get difficult in this world. Conflict is always with us in some part of the world, and though conflict brings tension, tension should never become fear or the inability to enjoy this wonderful world You have given us. I pray You will always be my strength, my rock, my salvation. Hear me when I call to You for help, Lord, for I know You love me.

~Toni Sortor

Cast your burden upon the LORD and He will sustain you; He will never allow the righteous to be shaken.

PSALM 55:22 NASB

GIVING GOD YOUR BURDENS

When we have a problem, our first thought is to contact a friend. In our world today, with so many technological advances, it is easy to communicate even with people who are far away. Just a hundred years ago, people waited days to receive a message from another town!

Certainly God desires that we help to bear one another's burdens and that we seek wise counsel. The trouble is that in doing so, often we fail to take our burdens to the One who can do something about them. We are called to release our cares to our heavenly Father. A cause with an effect is implied in Psalm 55:22—*If* you cast your burden on Him, *then* He will sustain you.

Sustain is defined by Webster as a verb meaning "to strengthen or support physically or mentally" or "to bear the weight of an object." Does it sound inviting to have the sovereign God of the universe strengthen and support you? Would it help if He bore the weight of your current trial? Our sovereign God is there when heartaches are taking their toll. He doesn't have a cell phone or an e-mail address, but He is always just a prayer away.

~Emily Biggers

Trials are medicines which our gracious and wise Physician prescribes because we need them, and He proportions the frequency and weight of them to what the case requires. Let us trust His skill and thank Him for His prescription.

SIR ISAAC NEWTON

OVERCOMING THE WORLD

*L*ord, You warned the disciples that the path lying before them was both steep and dangerous. During the course of bringing Your Word to the world, they would become the first martyrs of the Church, hounded and persecuted to death on all sides. Still, You urged them to be happy in this life. Although the world would treat them wickedly, You had overcome the world, and Your salvation was theirs forever. The power of the world is no match for You, and because of Your sacrifice, all it can do to us is kill the body and free the soul for eternal life with You.

~Toni Sortor

These things I have spoken unto you, that in me ye might have peace. In the world ye shall have tribulation: but be of good cheer; I have overcome the world.

JOHN 16:33 KJV

Wisdom

"My sheep listen to my voice;
I know them, and they follow me."

JOHN 10:27 NIV

LISTENING VS. TALKING

*I*t has been said that the Lord gave us two ears and one mouth for a reason: We need to listen twice as much as we speak. However, talking seems to come easier for most of us. Our interaction with others becomes the model for our relationship with the Lord. We can become so busy talking to Him during our prayer time that we forget He has important wisdom to impart to us!

Jesus is our Good Shepherd. As His sheep, we have the ability to distinguish His voice. But are we taking the time to listen? It seems much of our prayer time is devoted to reciting our wish list to God. When we stop and think about it, doesn't God already know our needs before we utter one word? We need to learn to listen more instead of dominating the conversation. God is the One with the answers. He knows all things and possesses the wisdom we yearn for.

Learning to listen takes time. Do not be afraid to sit in silence before the Lord. Read His Word. He will speak softly to your heart. He will impart truth to your hungry soul. He will guide you on the path you should take. Listen.

~Julie Rayburn

A loving heart is the truest wisdom.

CHARLES DICKENS

Looking in All the Wrong Places

*E*mbracing wisdom is not difficult for a child of God; finding it is harder. In our search for wisdom, we often chase after it in the wrong places. The evening news may give us the facts, but its interpretation of the facts is often flawed. Professors try to build wisdom through the teachings of knowledge, but a wise student carefully evaluates any conclusions a teacher draws from the facts. Only You are the perfect source of wisdom, Father. You give it to us liberally when we ask for it, never considering us stupid or leading us astray. You have given us Your Word as the best school-book of true wisdom.

~Toni Sortor

Do not wear yourself out to get rich; have the wisdom to show restraint. Cast but a glance at riches, and they are gone, for they will surely sprout wings and fly off to the sky like an eagle.

Proverbs 23:4–5 niv

Losing Interest

*E*very season of dangerous weather brings uncertainty. Normally meteorologists can track a storm's progress, but even if everyone is told to evacuate early, not every possession can be taken or protected. The aftermath of hurricanes, tornadoes, floods, and other natural disasters proves that possessions can be gone in seconds.

Some people stake their identities in acquiring possessions. Others live to make names for themselves. Even living for family members and friends can feel unsatisfying and empty.

Having money and possessions isn't wrong. Even having high-priced possessions isn't wrong. But there is something missing when our desire for wealth outweighs our desire for God. We may hold on too tightly to things that don't have eternal value and not cling closely enough to the One who does.

God has asked us to use wisdom as we work for Him. Wisdom plans for the future, but it also recognizes that even plans fail. Finances and storms come and go. Our trust in God can be a firm anchor.

~Kate E. Schmelzer

God, grant me the serenity to accept the things I cannot change, the courage to change the things I can, and the wisdom to know the difference.

REINHOLD NIEBUHR